TO A

SECRET

FEAST

~

SELECTED

POEMS

JOUMANA HADDAD

SELECTED POEMS

Invitation to a Secret Feast

EDITED WITH
AN INTRODUCTION
BY KHALED MATTAWA

ACKNOWLEDGMENTS

The poet and editor are grateful to
Banipal: A Magazine of Modern Arab Literature (UK),
Kalimat: A Magazine of Modern Arab Literature (Australia),
and *Meena Magazine* (USA) for publishing earlier versions
of some of these poems.

TUPELO PRESS

Tupelo Press
Post Office Box 539, Dorset, Vermont 05251
www.tupelopress.org

Cover and book design by Josef Beery

To the seven women
who live in me.

CONTENTS

Introduction   *i*

Lilith's Return 2004

Prologue   3
Beginning Again   6
Song of Salomé   8
Song of Nefertiti   9
Song of Balkis   10
Lilith's Return   11

I Have Not Sinned Enough 2003

The Panther Hidden at the Base of Her Shoulders   23
Duet   26
My Poem   28
Slow Down   30
Two   32
Chance   34
Blue Tree   35
Adrenaline   36
My Lover   40

Two Hands to the Abyss 2000

Your Homeland Is This Burning Night   45
I Have Not Sinned Enough   49
Bad Habits   50
Wet Face   52
Mere Shadows   53
Who Will Steal My Forest?   55
On the Playground in My Head   56
Identity   57
Devil   58

Invitation to A Secret Dinner 1998

I Have A Body   61

Then I Lost Him   62

I Am A Woman   64

Invitation To A Secret Feast   66

Don't Let It Linger   69

Harvest of Non-Memory   70

I Don't Remember   72

No   74

When I Became Fruit   75

About the editor   79

INTRODUCTION

Joumana Haddad belongs to a generation of Lebanese writers who began to publish after their country's civil war (1975-1992). Understandably, much of this writing sought to reconcile individuals and the nation with the years of harrowing violence they had experienced. One can say that Lebanese literature, particularly the novel, conducted a kind of truth and reconciliation commission on the war. Writers chronicled damages wrought upon civil life and individual psyches and offered lenses through which a new nation rising from the ashes of war might be seen.

Lebanon has been, for almost two centuries, one of the engines of Arab modernity. The country's sectarian mix, unusual for the rest of the Arab world, gave birth to a cosmopolitan atmosphere that made Beirut the Paris of the Middle East. Indeed after World War II, when Cairo emerged as the capital of the Arabs' unified political aspirations, Beirut provided a liberal space where divergent points of view converged. Political exiles from all over the Arab world found both refuge and publishers in Beirut. At least a dozen newspapers flourished and twice that many magazines. During the 1950s and 60s literary reviews such *Shiir*, *Al-Adab*, and *Mawaqif* guided Arabic literature and thought.

The war interrupted Beirut's centrality in Arab letters, but it hardly broke the city's creative spirit. Poets and novelists continued to publish during the war. In fact, during the war more books were published in Beirut than in several Arab countries combined. The end of the war allowed new literary life to emerge, one that addressed the important existential questions arising out of that legacy of turbulence.

The country and its writers were seeking answers. How does the phoenix rise out its ashes? How many phoenixes are there? The phoenix of the nation, the phoenix of the tribe or sect or region, the phoenix of the self—on which of these should one concentrates one's energy? The end of the war brought its own problems as well: inflation, unemployment, government corruption, and general disaffection. Many were disappointed by the country's new shape, dominated by Syria, threatened by Israel, and financially choked by global business, where national character was de-emphasized for political and commercial reasons. Some homesick Lebanese who left during the war returned; some left after the war.

For women writers in the two generations before Haddad's, the problems that led to the war remained unresolved. In novels, Etel Adnan, Hanan Al-Shaykh, Hoda Barakat, Ghada Samman, Mai Ghoussoub, and Emily Nasrallah highlighted Lebanon's social and economic inequities, which placed stringent limits on self-determination and self-expression for both men and women. They also critiqued the sectarian divisions that forced individuals into imposed identities and which lured the country to rely on leaders whose power stemmed from their ability to divide the nation rather than unify it. These novelists also emphasized that the emancipation of women cannot be separated from the social context. They denounced the weakness of men who, in the perpetuation of war, found a way to maintain power over their surroundings. These leading Lebanese woman writers promoted strengthening women's power-share in society to mitigate various forms of oppression endured by women and men alike.

~

Joumana Haddad's poetry emerges from such victories and devastations. Haddad was born in 1970 in Beirut, the first of two children born to Attallah and Mary Salloum. She is the author of four books of poetry: *Daawa il Ashaa Sirri* (*Invitation to a Secret Dinner*, 1995), *Yadan ila al-Hawiya* (*Two Hands to the Abyss*, 1998), *Lam Artakib ma Yakfi* (*I Have Not Sinned Enough*, 2003), *Awdat Lilith* (*Lilith's Return*, 2004). Long in love with languages, Haddad writes in French, speaks and translates from English, Spanish and Italian. She has published translations of a volume of poems by Emanuel Minardo, a novel by Antonio Ferraro, and an anthology of modern Italian poetry. She has edited and translated an anthology of Lebanese poetry into Spanish and compiled an anthology of 150 Twentieth Century poets who committed suicide.

Raised in a literary household, Haddad began publishing stories and poems in her teens in French publications in Beirut. Starting college at the age of 16, she went on to earn a master's degree in biology from the Lebanese University and a postgraduate diploma in literary translation from Université Saint-Esprit de Kasilik. She is completing a Ph.D. in translation studies at the Sorbonne. Editor of the cultural pages of the prestigious Lebanese daily *An-Nahar*, Haddad is the the first woman to occupy such a position in any leading newspaper in the Arab World.

She was recently brought on to administer the newly established Arab Booker Prize.

During the civil war Haddad attended Maronite/Catholic schools, but was often home-schooled by her mother due to constant interruptions. Her interest in literature finds in roots in her father's large library and his voracious reading. During her childhood and teen years, she read almost exclusively in French, and her first writings were in that language. Like many in her generation in the Arab world, she did not identify with the traditional modes of Arabic poetry. Preferring modern prose and prose poetry, she began to write in Arabic as well as French. In her twenties Haddad discovered modern Arabic poetry and found kindred voices and influences among the Shiir magazine group, who were spearheaded by Adonis (Ali Ahmad Said), Ounsi El-Hage, and Yusuf al-Khal. Almost immediately, she switched to writing poetry in Arabic.

Haddad's switch to Arabic was not a conscious nationalist gesture, but it registered a desire to root herself within her country's primary literary tradition. The choice of Arabic is significant as a sign of reaching out. It is important to note that Haddad and her family never left Lebanon during the war or after it. Combining these two seemingly innocent choices—staying put and writing in Arabic—we find that Haddad's choices amount to an expression of hope and commitment to her country.

~

Though informed and empowered by the works of her feminist predecessors, Haddad's poems do not address the social and economic ills of her society. Most significantly, the poems do not deal with the poet's direct experience of the civil war that lasted for seventeen years. Historical time does not factor in Haddad's poems, nor does any specific element of her region's history or social make-up. Is this detachment a means of recuperating from a personal trauma suffered on a national scale? Or are we wrong in seeing this lack of explicit commentary as detachment?

Arab literature, especially poetry, has long wielded a great deal of influence. Historically, Arabs have countenanced the power of words. It was, after all, the revelation of the Quran to Muhammad that set the Arabs on the road to glory for centuries. Of the treasures they hold dear from that golden age, none is as valued as poetry. The onset of the modern Arab awakening was more a literary renaissance than anything else. Beginning with the neoclassicists writing in the late 19th Century, poets felt it their duty to utilize their art and denounce colonization, and endorse social and economic reform. As the Palestinian cause became the nexus of Arab solidarity in the 1950s, committed literature championed by nationalists and leftists alike became the dominant mode. The defeat in the 1967 Arab-Israeli War and the onset of the Lebanese civil war rang a death knell over "instructive literature."

The Lebanese feminist writers mentioned earlier, and their sisters throughout the Arab world, had presented a parallel version of what ought to be done. They also methodically outlined the failure of both "progressive" and "reactionary" forces in the Arab world as an outcome of their societies' failures to uplift their own women from a denigrated state.

Beginning with the Shiir magazine group, there has been a streak in Arab modern literature that resisted politicized writing. The Shiir group aimed to promote literature that generated an internal sense of freedom to combat the external repressive forces of religion, society, and politics. Literature to engage and promote individual ideas might play an important social role by fostering imaginative thinking, they argued. This rich and controversial vein in modern Arab writing promoted quest, and a concomitant refusal to accept present reality. It encouraged a poetry of imagined time and place rather than real time and place. Only an open and completely free imagination can muster the courage to face its own failings and society's as well.

Haddad braids two strong contrarian currents: feminism and the estheticist strain of Arab Modernist poetry. Though "not a feminist" because she is wary of all ideological discourses, she benefited a great deal from the voices of other feminist writers. Like them, she recognizes that there is a serious problem of communication between men and women, ruled by a struggle for hegemony where domination is an ideology in itself. Haddad's poetry expresses her refusal to live in relationships where she is controlled. Haddad's poetics fall squarely within the conceptions of the Shiir poets who brought her into the fold of Arab poetry. "I don't want to be besieged in one language, one manner, one body, one name, one field of expertise," she states. The aim is "to turn away from the traditional prescriptive definitions, to invent a self with maximal freedom, without lugging with me what I was, what I believed, what I did previously, as if they are prisons chasing me into the future." From the outset Joumana Haddad's poems declare the poet's female consciousness and announce that her poetry is female-centered if not female-centric. The poet's ferocious and almost tactile femaleness within a patriarchal culture is paired with a contradictory, genderless desire to create space for creativity, original thought, and experiences.

•

But how does one write one's femaleness exactly? Haddad, who operates from within the center of her culture and works as an editor of a mainstream journal known for poise and circumspection, allows her poetic voice free range. "Innocence," Haddad states "is honesty with oneself and others." And honesty in poetry has to allow for audacity and fearlessness. An admirer of French writer Helene Cixous and Austrian novelist and Nobel laureate Elfriede Jelinik's work, and well versed in the work of George Bataille and de Sade, Haddad, like her iconoclastic influences, acknowledges and struggles with the absurdity of social clichés and their subjugating power. The social cliché penetrates the most private spaces, especially the erotic realm where men and women lay claim to each other on the basis of power rather than on the fulfillment of mutual needs and wants. From the onset of her poetic career, Haddad has focused on the most volatile zones of human relationships—where life reaches its apex and confronts death and where emotions often turn into their opposite.

Haddad's poet-speaker seeks union with her lover, but fights to maintain personal sovereignty with cunning, boastfulness, generosity, and tenderness as befits the encounter and suits her needs.

> *I have a body on the bottom of the ocean waiting.*
> *I have a body like a volcano…*
> *volcanoes that sound the arrival to heaven…*
> *I have a body for you, my love,*
> *a tomorrow and an eternity.*
> *Tomorrow from which you'll arrive to me,*
> *and an eternity in which the shell opens*

> *with all the slowness I desire,*
> *all the slowness*
> *you are capable of.*

The above passage is from "I Have A Body," an early poem. At the bottom of the ocean, the body is hiding and secretive. But this restrained discrete body is also hellish. Its heaven will declare its inception with the eruption of volcanoes that will not simply explode and disappear. Here Haddad sets up the dynamics of desire. She'll not agree that these dynamics are female, only that they are hers, and in them we find patience sitting comfortably alongside unspent energy. The patience does not render the poet-speaker humble. She spends time in exploration with lips that "singe" and a tongue that takes. When the beloved arrives, he is not served. He is asked to muster his strength and participate with keenness and patience while the speaker's leisurely desire commences.

Haddad's second volume, *Two Hands to the Abyss*, include poems titled "Identity" and "Devil" indicating the poet's increasing self-awareness and need for more dramatized voices. In "Devil," the civil romantic encounter is an act of treachery.

> *When I sit before you, stranger,*
> *I know how much time you'll need*
> *to bury the distance between us.*
> *You are at the peak of your intelligence*
> *and I am at the peak of my banquet.*
> *You are deliberating how to begin flirting with me,*
> *and I,*
> *under the curtain of my seriousness,*
> *am already done devouring you.*

There is none of the tolerance we encounter in "I Have A Body." The embrace of the hellish is complete. The poet-speaker is now more dangerous for knowing how to cheat "intelligence" with a curtain of "seriousness." In "Identity" we encounter a more contrite speaker who is at once resigned and defiant. "*It's useless to change me,*" she states. "*This is how I am — / no time for guilt, / playing with fate and quick to bore/,*" she adds. But the life of abandon has its costs.

> *This is how I am —*
> *a silence to reassemble my parts,*

a slow terror to shatter me,
silence and terror to heal me from a wicked memory.
No hope that light will ever guide me:
I own nothing
except my mistakes.

In her third volume, *I Have Not Sinned Enough*, Haddad continues her exploration of the erotic through the use of symbols in such poems as "Blue Tree." She re-examines her belief in the primacy of the erotic as an inroad into human essence by revisiting the books she studied while pursuing a degree in medicine. The light mood in "Adrenaline" becomes playful in "My Lover," where poetry, embodied as a prototypical masculine figure, is championed as the poet's life long love. The poet shifts to third-person point of view in "The Panther Hidden at the Base of Her Shoulders." The experimentation with voice continues into "Duet" where a witty and lustful dialogue takes place.

The culmination of Haddad's work emerges in "Lilith's Return" where she finds in the mythical figure the appropriate symbol to embolden her and to broaden her examination of the erotic. Lilith, the anti-Eve, returns to rescue the world from the daughters of Eve, from feminine meekness and propriety. Lilith is flesh; she seeks to fulfill desires without inhibitions and aims to take desire into oblivion where self-knowledge and self-erasure conjoin. "Lilith does not wait to be chosen or assigned a role. She initiates and does not wait to be given. She takes. She is the desired gender who belies the false logic of equality between the sexes." Lilith, the poet writes, in the prelude of that volume, is "what man lacks so that he is not wracked with guilt, what woman lacks so that she may become." She is then the ideal for both woman and man. Through the persona of Lilith, Haddad's obsessions as a poet become a powerful, lyrical discourse. As someone who seeks freedom on terms that do not denigrate any part of her identity, Haddad finds great comfort and stands supported by the backbone of an indomitable figure. In doing so, she writes the most ambitious and powerful work of her career.

~

This volume includes selections from Haddad's four books of poetry, *Daawa il Ashaa Sirri* (*Invitation to A Secret Dinner*, 1995), *Yadan ila al-Hawiya* (*Two Hands to the Abyss,* 1998), *Lam Artakib ma Yakfi* (*I Have Not Sinned Enough,* 2003), *Awdat Lilith* (*Lilith's Return,* 2004). Haddad's deep French / Arabic bilingualism, whereby the poet composes in two languages or more that are constantly at play over possession of the same poem, challenging and informing one another, has allowed her to produce two versions of the same poem. Her French translations of her Arabic compositions take on new life and provide other versions of the poems. Haddad's own English translation of the poem "When I Became Fruit" diverges from the original Arabic. With the exceptions of Marilyn Hacker's translations which are based on French versions, the poems here are based on the Arabic versions. I am grateful to the other translators for contributing to this volume and to the poet for the opportunity to assemble her extraordinary work.

KM
Ann Arbor,
September 27, 2007

Lilith's Return

2004

Wildcats shall meet with hyenas; goat-demons
shall call to each other. There too Lilith shall
repose, and find a place to rest

ISAIAH 34:12-14

PROLOGUE

I am Lilith the woman fate. No male escapes my spell, and no male would wish to.

I am the double moon Lilith. The black can only be completed by the white, for my purity is the spark of debauchery, and my probing the beginning of the possible. I am the woman-Paradise who fell from Paradise, and I am the Paradise-fall.

I am the virgin, invisible face of the shameless one, the mother-mistress and the woman-man. Night, since I am day, the right side since I am left, and south since I am north.

I am the woman feast and the guests at the feast. They named me winged witch of the night and goddess of temptation, they called me patroness of disinterested pleasure. I was freed of motherhood to be immortal destiny.

I am Lilith of the white breasts. Irresistible my charm, for my hair is long and black and my eyes are honey. Legend tells I was created of earth to be Adam's first wife, but I would not submit to him.

I am the first who is never sated because she is the eternal bond, the deed and its reception, the woman-rebellion, not the woman-yes. I began to detest Adam the man and Adam of Paradise. I had grown bored and refused and strayed from obedience. When God sent his angels to retrieve me, I was dallying, dallying on the shores of the Red Sea. They wanted me and I did not want them. They molded me to be molded, but I refused to yield. They sent me down into exile to become the pain of banishment. They held me captive to the earth's miseries, and made me prey for the most dreadful shadows. I was food for ferocious beasts. When they expelled him, Adam, my husband, became alone. Lonely and whimpering, he went to his god who created a woman for him from his rib, named Eve. He made her to expel death out of Adam's heart, and to perpetuate the race.

I am Lilith, the first woman, Adam's partner in creation, not the rib of cowering. When I could no longer stand my husband, I left to inherit my life. I instructed my messenger, the serpent, to tempt Adam with the apple of knowledge.

I am the woman-woman, the goddess-mother and the goddess-wife. I ovulated to become the daughter and the temptation of all time. I married truth and myth to become the two. I am Delilah, Salomé, and Nefertiti among women, and I am the queen of Sheeba, Troy's Helen, and Mary Magdalene.

I am Lilith, the chosen wife and the banished wife, night and the bird of night. True woman and woman-myth, Ishtar and Artemis and the Sumerian winds. The first languages narrate me and the tomes explicate me. When my name is mentioned among women, prayers and curses rain upon me.

I am the female-darkness not the female-light. No interpretation will account for me and no meaning will wrestle me down. Mythology has stamped me with evil and women have accused me of manhood. But I am not a man-like woman or a woman-toy. I am the fulfillment of incomplete femininity. I do not declare war on men, and I do not steal embryos from women's wombs. I am the desired devil. The urn of knowledge and the seal of love and freedom.

I am the two-genders Lilith. I am the desired gender. I take and am not given. I bring back to Adam his truth, and to Eve her fierce breast so the logic of creation is appeased.

I am Lilith, the adversary-creature, the adversary-wife.

What man lacks so that he is not wracked with guilt, what woman lacks so that she may become.

hm, km

BEGINNING AGAIN

God created woman in his image,
created her from raw earth,
created her from the idea of herself
Lilith, in whose eyes you see love lost
or love abandoned,
Lilith, huntress and hunted
Lilith, who coos like a dove to tame the lion
who makes laws and breaks them,
who is both queen and commoner
who stands at the earth's center
and watches it turn slowly round her
who takes to herself the cypress, the dusk,
the far reaches of the sea,
who is lovely as a cloud, drab as a cloud,
who has no time for summer weeping
or for the tears of autumn,
who binds her men, then weeps for their release,
who is nameless to us
who dresses like a whore
whose past lies in her dreams, whose future
already shines in her mind's eye,
who is strong in her womanhood, and therefore mild
who aches for love but finds no pleasure in it,
who eats the sky and drinks the moon like milk,
who is one minute in your arms,
the next a distant shadow
who is dawn light, whose nakedness
can only be seen by those who do not look,
free woman, woman in chains,
woman who is free even from freedom,
the place where hell and heaven meet in peace,
desire itself and desire for desire,

Lilith, a tree bowed by the weight of its blossom
Lilith, a lightning-strike on the edge of the abyss
Lilith, tender in victory, powerful in defeat,
Lilith, freedom from need and freedom from certainty
Lilith, who speaks for any woman,
hot for choice, who saw but never chose
Lilith, who chose but never put to waste
except when waste allowed the better choice
who speaks for every man, quick to betray
her sex, quick to betray, whose thousand cuts
are more tender than a thousand kisses.
Lilith, pious sinner, poet-demon, demon-poet,
find her in me, find her in dreams,
find her and take from her
whatever you want, take all, take
everything, it will never be enough.

dh

SONG OF SALOMÉ, LILITH'S DAUGHTER

I do not fear Satan
for Satan dreams me.
Each time I shut my eyes and sway before the mirror
he sees me.
Satan does not frighten me
and I will dance on Herod's red ashes.
I will drink the wine of virgins' hands.
I will kiss the mouth of my beloved's head so that death smiles at
me one last time.
O my adored and perfect one,
master of deserts and tamer of hyenas,
do you not hear your guillotine,
my heart,
calling to you?
Come, John,
I am the necklace betrothed to your slit throat.
Come and baptize me with the sun that bronzed you.
For you alone have I returned:
Let your blood which I spilled mark the path for you.

mh

SONG OF NEFERTITI, LILITH'S DAUGHTER

The lovely one has come
with the sun's sap beading on her lips
and the stars crowning her forehead.
She has come, the beauty with the burning gaze
whose absence is tyrannical,
whose appointments are unknown,
whose palm is peopled with forests and birds.
The dark lioness has come
with the charm of her eyes which kohl discloses
and with Egypt's flowers blooming on her chest.
Come, then, O peoples,
come forward from the East and the West.
Give offerings and sacrifices to your mistress.
And thou, Akhenaton, rejoice
for your nocturnal bride has arrived:
Leap into her bed,
soften her, arouse her, set her aflame.
She returned from her slumber
so that night will watch over you.

mh

SONG OF BALKIS, LILITH'S DAUGHTER

I am the queen of Sheba,

wise woman among the wise and snare for the careless.

The hothead sent his hoopoe to abduct me.

My perfumes preceded me to his dwelling.

My shifting sands imprisoned him

and he could not weaken my fortresses.

I am the valiant horsewoman.

The odor of nard precedes me, the stags follow me.

I rule my realm justly.

I vanquish humans and djinns.

I torture the replete to feed my starving lovers.

Mine is the fishhook of sleep and of waking.

The call-up of armies is mine, and my domain is their abode.

I am the delectable chosen one

whose voice is darkness and sugar.

I return to give Solomon his ring

and take back my throne.

mh

LILITH'S RETURN

I am Lilith, the goddess of two nights returned from her exile.

~

I am Lilith, returned from the prison of white oblivion, lioness of the master and goddess of two nights. I gather in a cup what cannot be gathered, and I drink it. For I am the priestess and the temple. I do not leave a single drop for anyone, lest they think I have had enough. I copulate and multiply myself to make a people of my own, then kill my lovers to make way for those who have not yet known me.

~

I am Lilith the forest woman. I never knew any waiting worthy of my desire, but I have endured lions and pure-bred beasts. I impregnate all my ribs to weave the tale; I draw all the voices in my womb to gather my followers. I eat my body so they will not call me starved and I drink my water so I am not thirsty. My tresses are long for the winter and my coffers have no ceiling. Nothing quenches me and nothing fills me, and I return to be the queen of the lost on earth.

~

Long are my tresses,
far
and long
like a smile fading in the rain,

slumber after pleasure reached.
My shivers are scars sometimes,
and the gleams of the blade, at all times.

~

I am the guardian of the well and the nexus of contraries.
Kisses on my body are the scars of those who tried. From
the flute between the thighs my song rises, and from my
song flows the curse, water on earth.

~

Goddess of two nights, convergence of contraries,
I rise only in darkness
and climb only abysses.
I stand only on the threshold
and return only from death.
I guard the well.
No sigh will obey a throat
except when washed
with the ash of my fingers.

~

I am the desired she-lion Lilith. The hand of every maiden,
the window of every virgin. The angel of the fall and
the conscience of light slumber. Daughter of Delilah,
Magdalene and the seven fairies. From my lust mountains
rise and rivers break. I return to maim the sprigs of virtue
with my water and rub the ointment of sin on the wounds
of deprivation.

~

From the flute of my two thighs my song rises.
Rivers stream out of my lust.
Why would the tide not rise high
when a smile glitters between my vertical lips?

~

I am the curse of past curses,
enticer of boats so the storm rages on.
My names bejewel your tongues when thirst befalls you.
Follow me as the touch follows the kiss
and take me like night on its mother's breast.

~

Because I am the first and the last,
the virgin courtesan,
coveted and feared,
disdained beloved,
and the veiled nude,
because I am the curse that preceded the first curse,
sin disappeared from the deserts when I abandoned Adam.
He wandered and shattered his perfection.
I brought him down to earth and lit the fig tree's flame.

~

I am Lilith, the secret of fingers that insist. I open the road
and uncover dreams and rend the cities of manhood for my
deluge. I do not gather two from each kind, but I become
them so the species will be purified of virtue.

~

All dreams are open to me.
I am the conscience of light slumber.
I wear dreams and shed them,
misguide the boats and let the storm fend for itself.
I scatter the sky with the cunning of a cloud.
No one gets my honey.
I have no home and no pillow.
I am the naked
who gives nudity the flower of its meaning.

~

I am the flight of screams and the seepage of perfume.
I came to rouse the jungle and the jungle's pirates.
I come to your springs to gush forth
with my blue hand covering everywhere.
You heard me before I began to tell.
You saw me before I rose from the East.
You loved me before I spilled.
I am rescue and I am the torturer.
I am in all directions.
How will you escape me when you escape toward me?

~

I am Lilith, the cup and the server.
I came to say:
One cup will not suffice me.
I came to say:
The server is blind.
I came to say:
Adam, Adam, you are busy with many matters but the need is one.

~

I am Lilith, the verse of apple. Books wrote me even if you
did not read me. I am unbridled pleasure, the renegade wife,
the fulfillment of lust that brings great destruction. My shirt
is a window on madness. Whoever hears me deserves to
die, and whoever does not hear me will die of regret.

~

I am the moon within.
My compass is astray, migration is my home.
No caller knocks at my door.
No house leads to my window.
And no window exists but the illusion of a window.

~

I am not the stubborn steed or the easy ride, but the shiver
    of the first seduction.
I am not the stubborn steed or the easy ride, but the debacle
    of the final regret.

~

I am Lilith,
Salomé's last dance and the fading of the light.
I climb your night stone by stone every time the sun of
    absence bleeds the horizon.
I climb to set a dream to the table.
I delve into your roving mind.
And I make room for my head in your sleep.

～

For my fires I climb the stairways of night,
and for your dreams
I seek not certainty but obsession.
Not arrival but the pleasure of non-arrival.
Your night is my ladder to me
and my hand to grasp what lies beneath imagining.

～

I was conceived under the sign of ecstasy,
she whose presence rises,
she whose tongue is a beehive,
she who is a cake, eaten and horded,
she who is the crying hunger,
she who guards Limbo with her life.

～

I am the arrogance of two breasts
budding to grow and laugh,
to want and be eaten.
My breasts are salty.
And so high that I do not reach them.

～

Two lamps insinuate two lights,
budding so that their mischief is forgiven.

~

I am the lascivious angel. Adam's first steed, corrupter of Satan.
The shadow of stifled sex and its purest scream. I am the shy
maiden of the volcano, the jealous because I am the beautiful
whisperer of the wilderness. The first Paradise could not stand
me. I was expelled to sow conflict on earth and to arrange the
matters of my subjects in beds.

~

I am Lilith, the light rising from the earth, body of
  abundant delusion.
Take the lion's mane off your head and wear my cloud.
Let your one summer be
a kiss that lingers on a throat
and an embrace that drizzles on the threshold.

~

My thighs are the gates to the confessional of the idle.
There is a soft death between them
so that Satan feels at home.
My thighs are the bars of the liberated prison.
They are the treachery of road robbers and sin's journey
  after it is spent.
Will any arrival occur while I am still the body of
  abundant delusion?

~

I possess Balkis's throne and Cleopatra's crown,
Narcissus's book and John the Baptist's head.

I have nothing with which to drape myself except my mouth.
My sex is quarantined in the depths of my head,
held prisoner so that it never stops demanding.

~

I am the yearning of the wheat fields.
The harvesters carry their sickles
to gather me, to braid me, to spread me, to return me to myself,
to be the ax and the woodsman,
bread and hunger and the satiation of the table that
   never stops hungering.
Bring the moon of your exodus so that the sun of my fruit will shine.
Bring your cruelty to sail the soft waiting,
and your branches for their share of grass and drowning.
My river will not flow
until a tree leans toward its banks.

~

I am the fate of the wise
gushing, mischievous, known and hidden.
The books wrote me and you did not read me.
This is my vision.

~

I, the goddess of the twin nights, the destiny of the wise. The union
of sleep and wakefulness. I am the fetus poet. I slew myself and
found her. I return from my exile to be the bride of the seven days
and the destruction of future life.

~

I am the seducing lioness. I return to slay the prisoners and rule the earth. I return to mend Adam's ribs and rid the men of their Eves.

~

I am Lilith, returned from exile to inherit the death of the mother I birthed.

hm, km

I Have Not Sinned Enough
2003

THE PANTHER HIDDEN AT
THE BASE OF HER SHOULDERS

Her hair is farther than last minute's pleasure, and in her
smile a thousand promises that do not stop the rain. Her
colors are a palette of tremors, sometimes shadow-scar and
sometimes knife-bright. No postman stops at her door since
she is not known to have a place to live in. She is not known
to have an end either, since she is free as a tree.

And like the tree, she climbs.

Come
Gather her up in torrents in your eyes

∼

Her garden, fortress exhaling intrigues, sweet death sniffing
out game. The devil feels at home there.
Looks cannot capture her, nor chalices. Woman of fog, of
uncertainties and fantasies.
Woman of falling, also.

On her skin shifts an infinity of unknown continents. Each
pebble is a false oath, smooth as waiting seen from afar,
and each hand each morning is a journey. But O how many
horizontal trajectories, and what little climbing!

Come
Nail your summits to her abysses

∼

Modest, she takes refuge in obscene words, insolent to
the point of blushing when crying out her flame. Amateur
warrior, career Amazon, she fires off words like arrows and
her arrows return loaded with prey.

She speaks all night's languages but writes first of all with
her fingernails. On the body is where she writes. Cursed are
the fingers that cannot decode the sharp tones of her ecstasy.
From the plunging neckline of her moans arise music, songs,
whispers and murmuring. An erupting violin, she searches
out the note-carpenter who will know how to vibrate her
strings.

Come
Etch her shape into the memory of your palms

~

Greedy and clothed with mouths, she is made for tasting
and being tasted. Her lips are edible and her tongue an
interminable spoonful of delights.

Fond of delicate flavors, she indulges herself at will, but is
careful to remain hungry.
The forbidden, her head's clitoris...

And her belly? A wheat field where desire's bread glistens...

Bring your scythe, harvester!
Take, press, sniff, caress, roll up, unroll
Be the axe and the woodsman
Be one direction and the other

24

May your memory ripen the fruit
May your hand navigate in the fluid vigil
May your fingers quarrel over the moon and the drowning
For the stream only starts to flow when the tree bends over it
It is desire that moves mountains
Not faith

mh

DUET

– Your eyes have woven a strange light within my gaze...

– That's because you've awakened the wood and the sailors
  of the wood.

– It's so blue. Where am I?

– In my arms. There where your stream catches fire.

– And this moon on my throat?

– It's my night which wants to put its seal on your skin.

– A beginning?

– Beginnings.

– And why do you open up with your eyelids shut?

– The better to see your haste slather my waiting. To hear
  our lips alight.

– You and me, a flight of cries.

– You and me, the poem's migratory wings.

– For you, I'll be the bird and the hunter.

– You won't conquer me. I'll offer myself to your gun.

– I'll plant it in your heart until it's vanquished.

– It's only in losing that one earns his journey.

– How to arrive? You have the body of abundant illusion.

– Why arrive? Become the hand of enduring delusion.

– Your thighs, gateway to the purgatory of the idle.

– My thighs, prison bars which liberate.

– Woman, I'm thirsty, pour yourself.

– Let your names slake your thirst. They are drops on my lips.

– I will let the fishermen come to you.

– But the violin is still locked. Will you know how to unbutton it?

– I'll learn. I'll shake it like a tree until all its music flows on my tongue. I'll work it the way the goldsmith works his metal, the sinner his damnation. I'll learn.

– And you'll make me yours, brigand?

– Always and never.

– I like the shiver you wrench from my throat.

– Then come. The wine is at low tide without you.

mh

MY POEM

1

My poem is not long, not existential, certainly not romantic.
It's not loaded with sentiments, or virtues, or even muddled
thoughts. No one speaks there, or begins anything, there are
no kisses on the mouth. There are no metaphors, lost birds, or
old dreams sitting in the shade. My poem is not a poem.

2

My poem is a steel wire. I walk its tightrope, I'm its hostage.
It vibrates beneath me and threatens to unbalance me. I hang
on to it, I dangle there. It's my fear and my escape. Then all at
once it becomes rail, ladder, wrinkle, precipitous fall through
which I don't stop saying farewell to all the mountains leaving
without me.

3

It's always black around my poem. The moon shines with
its erasure, night overtakes night. The landscape is a sharp
pebble under soles, and each look is a wound. The darkness is
someplace and no place and there is no other shore.

4

My poem is a hand. The hand of the man I love. Arrow, bow
and prey at once. It caresses me, wants to possess me. I don't
belong to it. It knows that. It returns me to myself and carries
me without owning me.

5

I look for my poem and my poem looks for me. Seven pages
separate us, seven wells. The same fire sees us, the same metal
begins us. Tyrant, neither homeland nor exile, it's in every vice,
every shudder. Both of us are overpopulated by absences and

passers-by. "Here's your adventure," it tells me nightly. And I travel.

6

My poem is the color blue. Its threshold is covered with seaweed, its padlock is rusted, and its own water is enough for it. I am its vagabond, I wander on its liquid asphalt and sleep in its inky nooks. I am its flock of clouds, its moss, its skin warm as oncoming pleasure. Drunken skiff in a storm, lightning bolt that leads me toward the face which resurrects and multiplies me.

7

My poem is a time lapse. An infinitely prolonged wait. Unsettling minutes building up between two beginnings. Unexpected moment that tumbles walls.

8

I am not in my poem. I am not beneath those nails which ask me questions, in that pain persisting in every step, between those lashes closed to my cries. Because I am in the poem or I am not. And it is in me.

9

My poem is a man's sex draped with desire. Bridge stretched between the universe and me. Marvelous fruit that lives on my body. Eye which slakes my thirst and snatches me up in its whirlwind. I never want to come out of its rainy tunnel.

10

My poem is a road. It walks, walks within me.
And I follow it.

mh

SLOW DOWN

Slow down, impetuous man.
Don't rush,
slowly mend your nets.

Slow down,
coming and going are the same.
The water's journey starts from below, rising.
And my body –
trust me – when the time comes
will not escape your deluge.

Slow down,
open your fist,
polish your blue sickle,
count your nails and bullets,
subdue my strength with sharp patience,
wrestle down my belt, that foe of your hands.

Irascible man, slow down.
Don't panic:
What looks like a wall
is a door,
and your waiting is its key.
Boost your eagerness,
the ravenousness on your table,
your madness and gasping.
I want you erupted, blown up,
and an avenger
so I retaliate.

Get ready, reckless lion.
Let the earth rotate faster,

and let desire surprise the absence.
Then wait a little more
before you pounce on my expectations.
Slowly weave your starry gold
over the palimpsests of my breasts.
Slip further and forcefully from me,
and from my salt drag out the sea.
Moisten, but do not fall,
for drizzle is the true meaning
of the brushing waves.

Slow down
like a scar sliding on skin,
like an arrow in love with the bow
or an eye seeing itself
in the gusting winds of infatuation.
Half of me has become a fire caught in a glance.
My second half is a windowless sphere,
and my third is watching over the storm.
Slow down, slow down, my ruin:

I am an addict
to missed chances.

na, km

TWO

Embrace me
so that when I lose my heart's strength
you offer me yours,
so that when my roots dig deep
they'll reach your abyss,
so that if I waste my life
I'll find in you a wealth of lives and languages.

Embrace me
so that I become an herb that denies rocks their sleep,
so that you become a soft stone under an herb's shadow,
so that between us a river burns and others overflow,
so that I climb from my heights to meet you,
so that I discover that you are the climb,
so that you discover I am the drowning,
so that if I walk towards you
I will raise a bridge between perishing and light.

Embrace me
so that you crave picking me like an apple,
so that I shed you as a picked apple,
so that I inundate you with what you cannot attain,
so that I conjure for you a night and a cloud hovering above a night,
so that you forget I am the tree of your limbs,
so that you forget you are the limbs of a tree,
so that if life defeats me
I win back my life in you.

Embrace me
then release my hands
so that every time we are almost one,
we remain two
defying fate.

na, km

CHANCE

One touch is enough for a ripe fruit
to betray her mate, the branch.
One fall is enough for a cloud
to anticipate its destiny.
A shirt made of embers is enough
to cast out the cold from winter's fire.
Not one, but two, banks are needed
to imprison a river in its sleeping bed.
An apple, or the idea of an apple
for the tree to celebrate its femininity.
One rock,
one rock is enough,
for the spring to learn how to dig out its tomorrow.
A rainbow and the mirage of a smile
for a forest to burst under rain.
Impatient stars are enough
for the moon to announce the evening,
a shadow of a lake
for a bird to set the sun of her estrangement,
a single tear drop from a wanton flash of lightning
for the sky to be electrified with its glowing body,
an herb
and the whispering of an herb
to green the moon.
One chance is enough for the heart to change its calling,
and one man,
one man's night is enough, I say,
for me to be a woman.

na, km

BLUE TREE

When your eyes find my solitude
silence ripens into fruit
and sleep turns into storm.
Forbidden doors fling open
and Eve begins to learn the lessons of pain.

When my solitude finds your eyes
the tears of my desire grow and spill
like the tide rushing to its demise,
or a wave racing to no end,
a winter rain that falls in all seasons,
or like sap trickling in drops and sighs,
a sap hotter than pain,
a beginning that never ends.

When your eyes meet my solitude
I spill myself until I rain, generous
like two delirious breasts,
tender as a vineyard that ripens the sun.
Pluralized, I rain
until the grass of your love shoots out
high and unruly.
Your arrow will return to the bow
like a blue palm
seeking its roots among the clouds.

na, km

ADRENALINE

The chemistry book says
that when first I saw you
my nervous system
sent coded signals to my brain
and my glands released hormones of all kinds and colors—
messengers to my senses
setting them on fire,
and this is love!

My same oblong red book says:
if we are lovers
it is because of endorphins,
and I have to thank also
testosterone and luliberin,
and not to forget dopamine—
the crafty one who whispers in my mind
"Find the source of pleasure!
Find the source of pleasure!"
This thunderbolt of love is a scientific cocktail,
a biological reaction,
a rush of blood through veins,
an electrical charge into cells,
a magnet.

Norepinephrine is for yearning,
for nipples to pucker up.
Phenylethylamine enlarges the pupils
and makes my hand tremble when held in another's.
Oh yes, I forgot:
oxytocin is for attachment
and serotonin to outwit routine.
A for vasopressin—

that hellish invention! —
it's so that I won't bear another man
but you.

The dynamics are simple,
says my little book:
Pheromones of a special kind
released by the body on first contact
excite the grey matter
and cause numbness,
then a sweeping attraction
then a coercive craze
then a functional disorder
then an organic need then an addiction then a poisoning,
and this poisoning,
chemistry declares,
this poisoning is love.

$E=mc^2$,
my physics book says,
and if I find you wonderful,
incomparable,
and I can't see your faults and weaknesses,
this is because relativity rules the earth,
and like poisoning
relativity too
is love.

Clinics and laboratories,
numbers and comprehensive surveys
examine the phenomena of jealousy and passionate love,
study the incentives of enchantment and carnal desire,

unfold the mysteries of infatuation,
the hours of watching the cursed phone
until it rings,
the enigma of the throat tied in a knot,
desire when it sets one's dress on fire,
and that dizzying rush of flying high.
Adrenaline,
it's all adrenaline, my love:
the real romantic is the brain
as CAT scans have shown,
and it is in the head
not on the left side of the chest
that love is born.

My reliable science books,
reference works and encyclopedias
confirm there is no reason to wonder.
It's a matter of genes,
potions and equations.
There is no reason to wonder then,
but when I look at you
and then feel there is a heart within my heart,
and a heart within it and a fourth and a fifth
and so on without end,
like eternal ripples on a river's face,
and when your name, only yours, appears in them
without a question and without fear,
without explanation and without analysis:
a life is taken and a life is given
in the naturalness of a wild flower that grows
without anyone's insistence,
like a miracle beyond nature and logic,

and when I sleep in you like a tree sleeping in another tree,
and when by casting dice I grant you my whole being every day,
at that moment, I say,
this
and only this
is love.

ib

MY LOVER

He is tawny, his gaze towers, takes away my breath. His
eyes shine like postponed love. He hates wearing neckties,
high-sounding speeches, electoral campaigns, and all kinds
of social hypocrisy. He is hunter, prey, and in-between. He
does not believe in gender equality. He enacts his laws
when alone, and when in groups breaks them. He has not
discovered that the earth is a flat orange, but he knows
that it revolves around him. He is sly and will not disclose
his age. He likes the color blue, the beginning of night,
and the end of the sea. He goes against logic, against the
sun, against poets. He is more important than Napoleon,
Marilyn Monroe, NASA, cell phones, more important than
the summit of Everest, email, cherries, and the Eiffel Tower
at night, and especially more important than himself.

He is a beautiful loser, and strong in defeat. He is conceited
like a cloud, and humble like a cloud. He does not obey, is
never satisfied, never tame, and does not believe. He has
the heaviest sigh in summer and the longest tear in autumn.
He is not inhibited, rather he is crowded like a beehive and
luxuriant like a cypress. His feet are immersed in the wind.
He plays with light in the expanse of the stars. He pulls
his women by their hair, then weeps on their breasts like a
baby. He does not watch television and does not call things
by their names. He is irascible, ferocious, quickly bored. He
dreams of his past and remembers his future. He does not
bow to a king or to death, not even to a white rose, but he
kneels before the exalted heights of a woman's breast. He
is tender in his manly strength, masculine in his femininity.
He is not afraid of hating God, homeland, or family. He is
not afraid of loving God, homeland, and family.

He refuses to marry because he knows better. He is obstinate like an orgasm that does not want to climax. He burns like a river. He drinks the moon in a bowl of milk and eats the sky from the palms of my hands. He looms on the horizon and is not caught. He says to the mountains 'Move' and they move, and to time 'Get lost' and they get lost together. He wears a soft light, and wears his nudity for the ones who see without eyes. He is the bullet in Lorca's head, the gas in Plath's lungs, the water of the Seine that embraced the last Celan's body, and he is the messenger's long hair reaching the springs. He is womb and exile, sickle and the sickle's slash, desire and its desire. He is an apple tree laden with the lust of becoming, a scattered lightning on the shoulder of an abyss, incense diffused from the body of imagination. No one knows where he wanders. His surprises are stunning, and staggering his sighs. I wait for him with the pains of a prey and the allure of a seduced woman happy with her captivity. I wait for him to fulfill a rapturous pleasure, so that I may be, or not be.

My lover, have you recognized him?
It is poetry, my lion, and I am its lioness.
It is poetry; no other knife suits me.

ib, km

Two Hands to the Abyss
2000

YOUR HOMELAND IS
THIS BURNING NIGHT

1

Who could you be, woman, stranger?
Your masks that erase all features of brooding
are a blind window now.
Famished like lightning, you steal sleep;
and from your wild dreams, tremors flare.
You are haunted by the hell of your body
and your breach widens in the vessel.
How can your loneliness rest on the pillow of the heart
among your crowded days?
How does your sorrow drape eyelids,
and how do your dizzying nights
snatch your face from the abyss?

2

Who could you be when you are the banishment
of memory from touch,
of roots from escape,
you, dark dissolution like black clouds,
you, an obliteration like a self?

Lust sates your parched body
like a desert drunk with the thirst of its sands.
Your narrow land is wider than a lover's chest.
One drop of your nakedness
and the moon falls apart.

3

Woman, you were not born to a tree
and you did not mature with the seasons.
Your doors are closed,

but you are tender like an unfolding pleasure.
You leave life's orchard to wrap yourself in fantasies.
You prefer to walk among the stars
and there, you shed your water to reach your sins,
your head
deeply,
deeply
fragrant with images.

4

Your sky, remaining high above,
softens boredom
and endows it with the dark taste
of a vanquished horizon.

Tell me, woman, how can your imagination be trusted to
   safeguard your essence?
How do your desires conjoin at dawn
and inflame your longing for nudity?
Why does every sunrise wield its knife, stranger?
Why do you?

5

You lose yourself in your night
and in bygone crossroads,
but your shadow seeks your fertile hands
and staggers with you under the arch of pleasure.

You are a stranger, woman,
and you know
you'll fall under this shadow of yours

and over part of a wall,
then you'll wait for departure to consummate itself.

6
Your homeland is this burning night.
No suns will extinguish it.
Your drunken branches sway on the edge of presence
whenever
a hand
attempts
to conceal itself.

Stranger, your homeland has no name and no end.
Whenever arrival approaches,
your soul
pushes it away.

7
How strange you are, woman stranger!
Under your arm you carry your loneliness
which runs in the plains
seeking birds for the forest.
Your gentle loneliness
like a swelling breast that has not crossed
the threshold of imagination.

Where do you lay your star to rest
when darkness touches you?
Where do you shine, strange star?

8

Your paleness guards you
while frowning faces await you in the dark.
Your humors are scattered over the concealed trail
and your soul drifts at night towards her dissolution.

Sorrows are not your springwell, stranger,
nor your inland sea,
but the journey that mines the soul's gold.

9

Who could you be, woman, stranger, my soul?
They think you are a rebel
when you are only a lewd lust penetrating itself.
And what they think of as rejection
is nothing but the vertigo of the maze.

And because of the excess of masks, your face is effaced.

ib

I HAVE NOT SINNED ENOUGH

I was hung in life by mistake
and in spite of myself.
So not to fall off the edge of boredom,
I dedicated my hands to committing intimate sins.
I was never mistaken.
I loved and closed many doors
so not to grant anyone my absence.
I sinned on purpose.
I wanted to have worthy offences.
I walked for a long time with the shadow
and for a long time I lured pleasures.
There was not a mirage that I didn't follow,
not a fire that did not catch me.
But I have not sinned enough,
and a long time will pass
before I will weep as I should.
A long time will pass
before I will know how to corrupt my life.

ib

BAD HABITS

She says love is a gamble
and she always loses,
that it is a bad habit
she will not dare give up.

She says she is afraid of light
even though the night she has wasted was not little.
She says she is content in her solitude
and does not care for companionship.
Still, she falls from her cloud
whenever rain guides her to her land.

She says she is strong, but in vain,
and gentle despite herself.
Still, she feigns cruelty
because tenderness
like love
is a bad habit.
And so is silence
which she will never give up.

She says she is bored.
Not even good enough for sleep,
but she sleeps to remain like a fetus
drowned in the waters of oblivion.

She says she is a tired woman,
bleeding recklessness,
wishing never to heal.

She says she is a loser by nature,
a loser to deserve all her victories,

and that life is a bad habit
which she hopes to keep
with a little bit of will power
and a great deal of forgetfulness.

km

WET FACE

He had to nudge her clouds into motion,
to cart the mountain that hovers on wet glances,
to make a tempest and a night.
He had to distract her until dawn
and to drink up her pain.

He had to stab her death,
to wake her with the rise and fall of his whims,
   to die in vain.
But he was afraid of returning empty-handed,
and he feared her face, afflicted with chronic night.

He had to take her without caution,
to give her reasons to be rash.
It would have been enough to surpass her regret,
to suddenly appear and besiege her,
to call her so to reach her,
to invade her to preserve her laugh
from the wounds of the window.

It would have been enough to open the prison
   of his sky a little
for the water of her madness to spill out,
enough to free the bird of her sorrow
for both of them to soar,
to listen to the rustle of her absence
to find her love in the depths of his eyes.

ib

MERE SHADOWS

I pretend I am myself,
but unknown creatures live in me.
Eyes that are not mine see the world,
and other bodies walk about with my life.

I pretend I am myself,
but I am the known one, concealed.
My mines have not been dug,
my metals have not been polished.
What appears of me
are mere shadows you cast
and they act out my life.
You may think I live here,
but I have not yet arrived, and I am not about to.
There is no space for me to cross towards you,
no moon to meet with,
no night to fall into from the day.

I pretend I am myself,
but in my inexistence I wander.
Idleness there is an open invitation,
chaos still shepherds the seasons,
time has not yet become time,
and forms have not become forms.
Lips remain unchanged,
and clouds neglect to pursue their rain.

Free, I disappear in my mirage,
no identity to withdraw from,
no belonging to threaten me.
I multiply until the numbers tire,
and I am as ignorant of them as the sea of its names.

No one calls me,
no one knows me.
Only words
slowly
shape me.

I pretend I am with you all,
but other creatures live in me.
If I were not born yet
and my illusion has preceded me to you,
it is because I preferred to delay
until my moment arrived,
and those creatures that were you disappeared
and I became myself.

ib

WHO WILL STEAL MY FOREST?

I burn my green leaves
and warm myself.
I breathe out
and slip
with the thrill of falling into the enemy's embrace,
with the joy of accepting the torturer's judgment
and the ravenousness of sharing the murderer's face.

I flee
from innocent frailty to absolute weakness,
from sex to a desire that no sex can kill,
from my own wisdom,
from the ice of escape.
I find shelter in the land of a brazen angel,
in brimstone growing within its own secrets,
away from my cunning despair
to the shock of pain freed from all hope
like the prodigal daughter going on her last escapade,
to the wedding that follows the sun
where I will neither live nor vanish.

My spirit calls me toward a reasonable madness
that has ebbed and flowed through my life.
So I begin to sway from rebellion to passion
and from ecstasy to dissipation
completely unaware.

And here I am returning
to love
like the return of the she-lion to her mate the lion.
Who will steal the forest from me now?

km

ON THE PLAYGROUND IN MY HEAD

For a long time
I was their spear and its target
until the scream of sex
filled my loneliness.

For a long time
they did not know
that I shone with femininity
in the bed of childhood,
and that I learned
to steal my own treasures to become rich.
For a long time
they did not know
that my body mellowed with its honey sheen
and found its narrow path.

For a long time
I invented arts and practised my instincts as suited me.
I just played on the playground in my head.
And I flirted
and I dallied.
I refrained,
and then again I yielded.
For a long, long time
they sat in my imagination
and I devoured them
and they did not know.

ib

IDENTITY

This is how I am—
no time for guilt,
playing with fate and quick to bore,
promises betrayed with neglect.

It's useless to change me.
Certainty is a stranger to me
because of the panic love causes,
because of imagination,
because I'm only
fit
for laziness.

My dates are arranged in the last minute
or in premature withdrawals,
in a sun that does not suffice
and a night that never rescues,
in impetuous leaps between thirst and its slaking.

This is how I am—
a silence to reassemble my parts,
a slow terror to shatter me,
silence and terror to heal me from a wicked memory.
No hope that light will ever guide me:
I own nothing
except my mistakes.

km

DEVIL

When I sit before you, stranger,
I know how much time you'll need
to bury the distance between us.
You are at the peak of your intelligence
and I am at the peak of my banquet.
You are deliberating how to begin flirting with me,
and I,
under the curtain of my seriousness,
am already done devouring you.

km

Invitation to A Secret Dinner
1998

I HAVE A BODY

I have a body on the bottom of the ocean waiting.
I have a body like a volcano.
Waters lap its opening
so it would not fling its ecstasy before the arrival of love.
I have a body I do not know.
It could be a grain of sand
or a red fish
or a pearl in a shell.
But I will explore its taste
on lips that singe
and a tongue that takes
and volcanoes that sound the arrival to heaven.

At the bottom of the ocean,
inside bubbles of desire,
I have a body for you, my love,
a tomorrow and an eternity.
Tomorrow from which you'll arrive to me,
and an eternity in which the shell opens
with all the slowness I desire,
all the slowness
you are capable of.

km

THEN I LOST HIM

He resembles no one:
I drew him,
carved him.
I made him
then lost him.

I carry his silhouette under my arm at sunset
and begin searching for him.
No one knows him.
I gave birth to him in an hour of desperate revelation
from a hand resting on my cheek.
I raised him on easy tears and choicest words.
He is the ruler of a cursed dam,
master of an impending avalanche,
savior of my old covenant and destroyer of all future
  prophecies.
I drew him, carved him, made him.
Then I lost him.

He has no adversary.
He has deferred women since the beginning of time,
singular and numerous like the sex of men,
but he resembles no one.

He rose from the corners of myth,
lifted on the wings of ancient disappointments.
He leaves a land that becomes nations.
He tosses shells and they become destiny.
He adorns pain.
He follows the body with a speechless mouth
and glories in every utterance.
He praises at times, and at times denigrates,

and the gap explodes in tension,
and the shifting sands revolt
along with everything that hides under them.

An unhurried predator,
he knows he'll win.
He seals hunger, seals it with one hand,
and his other hands rove
deeper than the wellsprings of pleasure,
further than defeated desire.

He is the regret that never appears in mirrors
and the rescue that always arrives late.

Ah, how much pain,
how much more waiting,
how many more lying faces
of a lover who resembles no one!

I drew him, carved him, made him in my imagination
then lost him between two slumbers.

km

I AM A WOMAN

No one can guess
what I say when I am silent,
who I see when I close my eyes,
how I am carried away when I am carried away,
what I search for when I reach out my hands.

Nobody, nobody knows
when I am hungry, when I take a journey,
when I walk and when I am lost.
And nobody knows
that my going is a return
and my return is an abstention,
that my weakness is a mask
and my strength is a mask,
and that what is coming is a tempest.

They think they know
so I let them,
and I happen.

They put me in a cage so that
my freedom may be a gift from them,
and I'd have to thank them and obey.
But I am free before them, after them,
with them, without them.
I am free in my oppression, in my defeat
and my prison is what I want.
The key to the prison may be their tongue,
but their tongue is twisted around my desire's fingers,
and my desire they can never command.

I am a woman.
They think they own my freedom.
So I let them,
and I happen.

ib

INVITATION TO A SECRET FEAST

A woman in love is not torn apart by waiting. She can't feel fear even if she doesn't know the rest of the story. The story is you, and the rest will surely come along. She is sad because you've yet to leap out of her eyes, because you've yet to slide into her hands, because her tributaries have not surprised you. She is sad for you, because you do not know how many moons will glitter on her lips, how much gold will shine on her cheeks, and how on each corner of her landscape a new woman will await you.

A woman in love seeds her solitude with love, with winged desires and delectable chaos. She conjures the uninnocent shadows of others so that her fire's thirst is not slaked, for it's the others who fuel her waiting. Her hurried euphoria is a cold bed in the body's song. Her longing for you enslaves all that is rebellious inside her, unleashes the braids of all that is enslaved with her. Longing lives in her suspended Paradise, and she does not celebrate the wall, the enclosed women, or the contrived innocence. She has prepared a horde of reckless desires to celebrate your body whenever it arrives. She will not summarize, or suppress, or waste anything. She will take what is hers and what was not meant to be hers.

A woman in love awakes delusions and imaginings. A smile aimed at absence grants her an impossible presence, a guiltless, unyawning guilt. Creatures that resemble flowers will guide you to the road, and will cheer the miracle when you at last find the princess of storm. Longing seeps to the bed of a princess in love, from her clothes, from her lack of clothes however they conceal. Longing will rush in its search of you, rummaging through dusty images and empty shapes. Longing will seep from the princess's bed. It will convince poetry to be kind toward a planet that you fill, you and a few suns and insurmountable heat.

The woman in love is yours. You are her pole. In the palm of your hand her heavenly roots dig in. In her eyes she bears the call of fire and a promise of the undoing of quietude. Her pain resembles the love that came before the first love. You did not send fire her way, but what your lips do is a marvel, and what you have yet to make is miraculous still.

The woman in love is within you. You think you can make her disappear, but you only hide your sparrows, your thoughts and pleasures in her forest. At night, especially, and in the morning too, you invoke touch in her, the wellspring and the rush of breath. Whenever you truly reach out for her, she will snatch your past victories and disappointments and offer you your future sins.

The woman in love is coming toward you. Travel will not undo her. From her present, a dream will endlessly gleam to lure you to her windows, a dream that shields her from her impoverished waking. It will lift her away and will not land until it reaches your face.

The lover is yours, in you, toward you. In her sleep she swings between a great forgetfulness and many small ones. But she does not wake except to a desire for you that would not heal. She renders you a god whenever you see yourself in her eyes. She returns you as a man whenever she looks

into your eyes and calls out to you. Do not ignore her
invitation to this secret feast. The woman in love is ready.
She cannot bear the wait.

km

DON'T LET IT LINGER

I will be strewn on your bed
like fingerprints of fire.
I will be implanted in your night
and my day will spill out from your jar.
I will know your rooms by heart, word for word,
your verses line by line.
I will run and run in front of you
and I will catch the wind's hand and pull it along.

My mouth will slide from your forehead to your neck,
from your neck to that most significant crux.
I will unload my dreams on your shoulders
and you will let me wander.
Come along.

The earth is collapsing on me,
but I will not flee into myself.
Lust wants to taste me,
but I will not guide it to my home.
My dress is devouring me.
I will not expel it alone.
Come along.

You barge into my head
and I veil myself with fantasy and chase you.
Come, I won't call out to you again.
Come, cling to me
and don't waste my dizzy madness.
Beware not to let my fragrance linger.
Don't let it remain behind
once I am gone!

km

HARVEST OF NON-MEMORY

I allied myself with despair so that your voice will seep
from yesterday.

I want to avenge myself.

I have no need of you. My stubbornness is a wall between
my delusions and the corridors of memory.

Incapable of sin, incapable of virtue.

I want to crush you, but I am a drop of dew.

Downward, dear heart. We will seek no one's help.

The night sky is barren, don't ask me about the moon. He
is swimming in a bog. The cursed one lured him with her
vagueness. She appeared before him velvet-skinned from a
distance and he bound his pride and leapt. No, he did not
jump. He fell.

I reached you at the edge of the volcano and held you, but you
did not hold on to me.
I followed you to the cave, carrying light, but you buried the
keys of light.

The nymph fell in love with the ship's captain. The sea
will become her prison.

Everything comes and goes. Everything vanishes. Time has
come, time has gone, and I refuse to learn the rules of the game.

The world and I no longer gaze at each other. Has the time
come to harvest non-memory?

I wove for you a space of no-return, and I fused with
the earth and planted roots.

I awakened for you the winds of my madness, and they
spread on the carpet of wisdom and blew away.

Have I forgotten the language of clothes because of you and
your deeds?

You offered me a fig leaf to cover a nakedness that
resembles innocence.
You have rubbed the crystal ball, my Lord, and we
are now blessed.

Downward, dear heart, my heart.
No wave will crash on you.
Autumn will not weep over you on the breast of a tree.
No garland will kiss your grave.

Tomorrow is an implosion and the time of harvesting
non-memory has come.
I want to avenge myself of what I cannot do. Incapable of lying,
incapable of believing, incapable of the sun.

Oh, how the cold pains me with the tug of its aroused fingers.

km

I DON'T REMEMBER

I don't remember
that I undressed in daylight
for a man
whose eyes are closed.

I don't remember
that I ran like saliva
and he was an unattainable desire,
that I was ravenous with hunger
and he was an impossible bed,
that I was the conqueror
and he a resilient city.

I don't remember, don't remember
that I conquered a man like a storm
and he was the open windows that faced my weakness,
that I pounced on him like a fever
and his hallucinations swallowed my tongue.

I knew men's bodies as travel
and my body as arrival and easy farewell.

I knew that men's hearts are pairs of hands,
and knew my heart was a promise of asphyxiation
that remains false even when it wins.

I knew that men's arrival was a gentle flood
and their departure a temporary ruin.
I knew how to forget them even as they stormed the
    dust of memory.

I had never known a man
whose heart professed rupture like a foretold catastrophe.

I never knew a man
who could turn me
from an Eve into woman.

km

NO

I see you in daylight, an impossible moon,
and in my night a sun, unreachable.
So I refuse to love you.

In my mirror I see you, the silhouette of a tattered sadness
that my eyes hold captive.
And on my scattered papers I see you,
the traces of tears I have yet to shed.
And I refuse to love you.

I see you as a prohibited dream
that combs my innocent hair into sinful braids,
and when I awaken,
your luminous kisses drip
on my pillow
one star after another
to put out my shyness.
And I refuse to love you.

Because I love you
I refuse to love you.

Because my thirst for you is fire,
and because my heart does not deserve
the fate of a crazed moth.

Because I love,
and because you love me,
let your pride refuse my ashes.

km

WHEN I BECAME FRUIT

Girl and boy I was conceived under the shade of the moon,
but Adam was sacrificed at my birth,
immolated to the mercenaries of night.
And to fill the gap of my other essence
my mother bathed me in waters of mystery,
placed me on the edge of each mountain
and molded me in light and darkness
so that I become the center and the spear,
transfixed and glorious,
the angel of pleasures that have no name.
Stranger I grew
and no one harvested my fields.
I drew my life on a white sheet,
an apple which no tree gave birth to.
Then I split it and got out
partly dressed in red and partly in white.
I was not only in time or outside it,
for I matured in the two forests
and I remembered before being born
that I was a multitude of bodies
and that I slept for a long time,
that I lived for a long time.
And when I became fruit
I knew what awaited me.

I asked the wizards to take care of me.
So they took me.
Sweet was my laughter,
blue my nudity
and timid my sins.
I flew on a bird's feather
and became a pillow at the delirious hour.

They covered my body with amulets
and coated my heart with the honey of madness.
They protected my treasures,
and the thieves of my treasures
brought me silences and stories
and prepared me to live without roots.
I have been flying ever since.
I reincarnate in the cloud of each night and I travel.
I am the only one to tell myself good-bye,
the only one to welcome me.
Desire is my way and the storm my compass.
In love I do not drop anchor at any port.
At night I give up most of myself.
Then I embrace myself passionately when I return.
Twin of high tide and low,
of a wave and its sands,
of the abstinence of the moon and its vices,
of love
and the death of love.
During the day my laughter belongs to others
and my secret feast belongs to me.
Those who understand my rhythm know me,
follow me
but never rejoin me.

jh

ABOUT THE EDITOR

Khaled Mattawa is the author of three books of poems, *Ismailia Eclipse, Zodiac of Echoes,* and *Amorisco* (forthcoming from Ausable Press). Mattawa has translated five volumes of contemporary Arabic poetry and co-edited two anthologies of Arab American literature. He has received a Guggenheim fellowship, an NEA translation grant, the Alfred Hodder Fellowship from Princeton University, and three Pushcart Prizes. Mattawa teaches in the MFA Creative Writing Program at the University of Michigan, Ann Arbor.

THE TRANSLATORS

This volume includes the works of several translators, whose names are indicated by their initials at the bottom of each poem. The translators who contributed to this volume are:

Najib Awad (*na*)　　　　Khaled Mattawa (*km*)
Issa Boullata (*ib*)　　　　Henry Matthews (*hm*)
Marilyn Hacker (*mh*)　　David Harsent (*dh*)
Joumana Haddad (*jh*)